GRAMMAR NONSENSE

AND WHAT TO DO ABOUT IT

ANDREW WALKLEY

HUGH DELLAR

WAYZGOOSE PRESS

CONTENTS

INTRODUCTION

At Lexical Lab, we promote what might be broadly seen as a lexical approach to teaching and learning. As a result, I've quite regularly come up against certain grammar fanatics who falsely characterise this as meaning we are "only teaching words", while also claiming we somehow lack the appropriate rigour needed for teaching grammar. These people often employ a very prescriptive view of grammar as right or wrong, and make statements like "you should never use *less* with a countable noun".

In contrast, a lexical approach to things utilises a descriptive way of seeing how language is used, a view that's been greatly aided in recent years by the availability of huge corpora — data bases of used language – and of computational tools that allow you to analyse these corpora. The analysis of real used language frequently proves that many prescriptive rules simply don't stand up to scrutiny.

The chapters in this book were originally written as blog posts on our website to highlight differences between the prescription and description of language. In this respect, there are plenty of forefathers (and mothers) to these chapters. For instance, I have seen Dave and Jane Willis talk about how *would* is far more common in talking about past habits than *used to*; Michael Lewis, the author of *The Lexical Approach*, would collect instances of native speakers 'breaking' EFL rules by saying, to give just one example, *'more easy'*; and Michael McCarthy, who has produced various grammars of spoken English, apparently produced a similar dissection of reported speech to the one in this book some twenty years ago.

I guess ultimately this is the most annoying thing: the fact that many of these so-called 'rules' were debunked years ago — often by the same people mentioned above using rigorous corpora-based research that revealed quite how lexical much used language really is. Language is in fact full of fixed groupings of words and with vocabulary and grammar so thoroughly intertwined, they often impose constraints on one another. However, even today, when we write coursebooks, we have to constantly refer back to the 'old' rules that have been passed down through the generations and which these days may be monitored / guarded by specialist 'grammar editors'.

Editors play an absolutely vital part in producing good material that others can use, but they sure as hell can be annoying and highly conservative at times! It is these ongoing clashes with editors over the many years I have been writing coursebooks with my co-author Hugh Dellar that provide the backdrop to the blog posts that appear as chapters in this book. Hopefully, it also takes these chapters beyond what previous authors have done in pointing out of discrepancies between reality and published 'ELT' rules. That's because I have also tried to consider how these discrepancies come about in the first place; how they are perpetuated; how an 'unknowing' student might perceive these rules; and how the rules play out within the methodologies of coursebook series, and how they are designed.

The chapters were, therefore, originally an opportunity to get things off my chest, and as a result, are often written in the style of the rant. However, in the end, I am also a teacher! And any good teacher will not just use a red pen and strike through things that are wrong (or they don't like!). Instead, they'll also point to alternatives and ways to improve the situation — or at the very least, pose questions for students to consider. To that end, even the chapters about grammar nonsense contain at least some suggestions for English Language students and professionals.

I've also included what I originally called 'grammar curiosities' — patterns and aspects of grammar that tend to go unnoticed and untaught in most ELT material. To be fair, there could have been more of these, but it turns out that rants are more fun to write, and the blog posts were initially written more for my own amusement than anything. Some of the same authors mentioned before have also written extensively on areas of grammar not covered in coursebooks. I might add to those a couple of others who have influenced me and who happen to be friends: Ivor Timmis and Ken Patterson. Ivor wrote a number of academic publications on grammar in spoken language. Ken (along with another friend Rebecca Sewell, who I worked with for many years) wrote a practice activity book on spoken grammar for DELTA publishing.

With each post I wrote, certain themes and fallacies emerged, such as:

- the intrinsic ambiguity of language and the need for tolerance to that ambiguity;
- the pressure to show 'development' and the over-complication of rules;
- the backwash of exams and error analysis;
- the question of what the appropriate size of a grammar focus should be — a McNugget, an olive, or something else?;
- the pressure to treat all grammar in the same way – in particular, the need for some kind of massed practice;
- the transformation fallacy – that the process in the speaker's mind is to take base forms and change their grammar to create a different meaning or emphasis;
- the repeated need to be presenting more grammar through providing examples and focusing on what students are saying – or trying to say.

Finally, I should also acknowledge my friend, co-author and co-founder of Lexical Lab, Hugh Dellar. While I was the one who actually sat and wrote all the chapters in this book, they are also the fruit of many exasperated and entertaining (and generally ruder!) discussions Hugh and I have had over the years on these subjects. He has also been a keen and necessary editor of my writing. This should also be explanation for the drift between the use of *we* and *I* that you'll see throughout the book.

Ultimately, whether you agree or disagree with these insights — and comments on the original blog posts did suggest some didn't! — what I hope you find here is someone who after thirty years still has a love of language, teaching and our industry — despite all his and its flaws.

Andrew Walkley

1

REPORTED SPEECH

IS THERE anything that is more bizarrely and unnecessarily taught in ELT than reported speech? There have been many times when my heart has sunk as I've faced 'the reported speech unit' – both as a teacher and as a writer. I've often wanted to disappear into a dark corner and weep! And there have been more than a few occasions when my students have clearly felt pretty much the same after they've 'discovered' the lengthy list of rules, done endless transformations and tried and failed to fulfill my insane requirement that they **repeat exactly** what their partners had just told them two minutes ago following all rules previously looked at!

The main thing that annoys me about reported speech is that the use of tenses, pronouns, time phrases and all the other guff isn't actually different to the way tenses, pronouns, and time phrases are used at any other time. As Michael Swan says in *Practical English Usage*, 'it is not necessary to learn complicated rules about indirect speech in English' (1995).

Unfortunately, Swan then goes on to give **six** pages of rules! Why? Because like most of us (and I'm not entirely innocent myself), he's trapped by exam grammar and traditions which see reported speech as a series of transformations where we literally transcribe what was actually said, word for word, into our report – and in constructing these new sentences, we move one tense back from the originals and make other appropriate changes to pronouns and time words – always with *the exact direct speech* in mind. That may be what students have to do in state exams, for example, and, consequently, is what we ask them to do all the time in our lessons. However, it is definitely **not** how things happen in real life.

In real conversations, it's rare to report all of the actual words we heard – and when we do, we tend to make a point of it:

> *I'm sorry, but you said – **and I quote** – "I will never do it again" – so why the hell am I picking up your shoes from the middle of the living room floor again!*

> *You said, 'I've not heard anything about that' – **those were the exact words you used!***

And, of course, there's no back shift of tenses, etc. Because of the need to be specific about the words people actually said, we use the exact words we heard! Not that this – or the phrases used to draw attention to this use – are ever taught, probably because they are suggestive of arguments, which as we all know simply do not exist in the nice, happy, shiny world of English Language Teaching!

When it comes to normal indirect speech, we usually just report the generality of what was said. We don't really transform things that we heard, but rather we tell a kind of story. That may be a story which includes a bit about what was said among other actions, or it may be 'the story' of a whole conversation, but in either case, what we do is use tenses (and pronouns and time phrases) in the same way as we would when we tell any other kind story that happened in the past. Yet when I have written examples for practice of *narrative tenses* such as these:

- *She said she **was feeling** unwell so she sat down and we got her a glass of water.*
- *He told me he **hadn't spoken** to anyone about it before.*
- *They said they **would** call back later.*

I have sometimes been told (by editors) that these were examples of reported speech and somehow **not** normal examples of past continuous (interrupted/unfinished action at the time of *her speaking and me hearing it*), past perfect (before the *he spoke and I heard it*), and *would* (future in the past)!

Let's push on with the idea that tense use in reported speech is no different to how tenses would be normally used. Logically, of course, if what we're reporting is still true, there's no need to use past tenses at all! So, the following, while 'reported', are all perfectly correct:

- *She said she**'s feeling** unwell. Can you get her a glass of water?*
- *He told me he **hasn't spoken** to anyone about it before.*
- *They said they**'ll** call back later.*

Furthermore, it's likely that the actual direct speech was different. The original version may well have been something like:

- *I feel really rough. I think might be sick.*
- *Honestly, I haven't told a soul about it. I've been carrying it about with me all this time.*
- *Don't worry. We'll have to come back this way anyway, so we can drop by again then.*

It can actually be pretty weird if someone really does report something word for word. For instance:

They said I didn't need to worry. They would have to come back later so they could drop by again then.

> OK. Thank you for the message ... though I'm slightly disturbed by the fact that you repeated their exact words!

Similarly, all the other rules about changes are largely redundant when you think about it from the point of view of just telling a story or giving some relevant information as opposed to doing a mathematical transformation in your head! Why, for example, would anyone use 'today' instead of 'that day' or 'the same day' unless they actually wanted to talk about *today*! Or use 'the following day' when they actually want to talk about 'tomorrow'? Why would someone use **I** or **We** when they are reporting what someone else has said? Yes, these 'mistakes' may occur when we ask students to do transformation exercises, but they are not mistakes that happen when a student is trying to convey their own real meanings. The exercises are designed to elicit these mistakes and we fail to realise this at our peril.

Which brings me to the last point: how these things are practised. Reported speech is rarely practised as part of a story, but nearly always as some interview which you listen to and then report. Has any teacher ever honestly listened to such reports and thought, "Yes, that all sounds very natural. What a good job I did with this"?

> "Hey, my friend he says [said], yes he said he is Spanish [was Spanish – remember it goes back], yes he said he was Spanish and he said he was a teacher and he said he'd got married last year, and he said he is [was] he was going to Cuba in the summer".

Just shoot me now!

It does make you realise, though, that a lot of what we say is basically the reporting of speech. How else do we find out that someone is Spanish, a teacher, got married last year and is going to Cuba in the summer? Yet when we put 'he said' in front of it, it becomes a whole new category of grammar!

It's nonsense. We know it's nonsense, right? But we're also sometimes trapped as writers and teachers by the grammar syllabus imposed by publishers, or a ministry of education, or simple tradition. What might be a way out here? Here are a few suggestions:

1. Let's just teach reported speech as part of normal tense teaching / narratives.

2. Correct the use of tenses, pronouns etc. in terms of the use of tenses rather than according to a rule of indirect speech – and do it when students are trying to produce real reporting.

3. Practise it as part of telling stories or talking about broken promises, etc.

4. Come up with some other context where you might typically report such as:

So what did the doctor say?
Did you speak to the landlord?
Did you speak to the teacher?

and then give answers in terms of general reports of the conversation rather than transforming *the exact words*. You will probably need to focus at least as much on the words these people typically use in these conversations as on the grammar.

5. If you *do* do transformations – and you might need to because of exams – don't confuse instructions about completing the exam task with rules for the real world!

2

REPORTED SPEECH – WHAT WE MISS OUT

THAT PREVIOUS CHAPTER on reported speech got quite a lot of discussion going when we first published it online, and it seemed that on the whole, there was quite a lot of sympathy with the view that many of the 'rules' about reported speech that are commonly taught are what we technically term 'guff'!

There were some dissenting voices and some interesting questions were raised, so I thought I would follow it up with some responses and also a look at some reported speech curiosities – things that don't often get taught, but that are incredibly common (or else that simply got me thinking)!

We're not saying don't teach it – just teach it differently!

So first, a response to the view that we DO need to teach reported speech because it works differently in some languages. The answer to this is that I agree we should give students the opportunity to learn 'reported speech', but I just think that the rules we might teach would be different.

As stated at the end of the last post, we could just teach 'reported speech' as a part of teaching tense meanings when teaching particular tenses (so we might have examples of reported speech when teaching the past simple, the past continuous, the past perfect, *will*, *would*, etc.). It might also come up when we're teaching the 'skills' of telling stories, and we could pick up on errors at other times in *any* lesson too – if (and it's a big if) they are genuine errors in the context that they're being used in.

Correctness and level

To begin with an example, in a recent online discussion, we were asked about the sentence *He definitely said he was a vegetarian.* We were asked what we would tell students about the use of *was*? Is *He definitely said he is a vegetarian* wrong? If not, and a student asks why the different tense here, what would you say?

I would say that we use the past tense here because the person is reporting their understanding of the situation **at a particular time** (when the original announcement was said), and that this feature is especially common when it appears the situation is different now (he isn't actually a vegetarian after all!).

In this context, using *is* could be said to be 'wrong' or confusing to a listener if there's now proof that he isn't actually vegetarian. However, as is so often the case, this is all incredibly dependent on context and the great problem with reported speech teaching is that we almost never **have** this context. Instead, we're just given mathematical transformations of single sentences.

The second issue is to do with the level at which we should make distinctions like these. To me, this particular issue is an Advanced or Proficiency level thing. And even then, we should really only be correcting students' use when we have the full context and that context can only properly come from students trying to report things in genuine ways for themselves. The good news, though, is that there are, in fact, lots of opportunities for this, such as every time they retell what they understood from a listening, which they're often asked to do, or simply just during the general conversation and banter between students in a class. I'm still not convinced it needs a special lesson.

He was like 'That's so stupid'

For many, the use of *like* to introduce reported speech is a bugbear, something to be ranted about and, if possible, stopped! Quite apart from the fact that this is like King Canute trying to stop the tide from coming in, I actually think disliking the use of *like* here is kind of misunderstanding the general nature of reported speech and what is actually being reported when *like* is used.

As we already established, when we report speech, we do not usually give an exact report of what was originally said. So if you wanted to report my last blog post, you could say, *Andrew said the rules of reported speech were stupid!* I think that would be a reasonable summary, but those aren't the exact words I used. Or you could say, *Andrew gave some examples of how we teach reported speech rules and he was like, 'That's so stupid'!* I would argue that the use of *like* here emphasizes that the direct speech is a summary of my feelings – not the actual words. It's basically what I was thinking, which is not the same as the actual words I used. It's similar, it's *like* what I said, but it's **not** the same!

Very often when people use *like*, they may even be reporting a thought or feeling that they're summarizing with a thing that we might typically **say** when we have such thoughts or feelings – *and I was like, 'Stop right there! I think they've got your point' but he still went on for another half an hour!*

She says and I go

One other way that we introduce reported speech, which often gets sidelined, is to use *say* (as opposed to *said*) and *go* and *went*. This again follows on from the idea of reported speech being something that forms a central part of telling stories or anecdotes. I use these words in the widest possible sense here, by the way, so your 'story' might be about how you missed the bus this morning.

When reporting things that happened, it is also not unusual for people to slip into the present tense. The reason given for this is that it adds immediacy or drama. I don't know if that is actually a choice that people consciously make, but whatever: it happens. I think in the case of second language users, this is often done because it's cognitively easier – essentially no rules are being employed apart from our most familiar base forms. Should this be a thing to correct, then? Should we really be encouraging the use of *said* or *told me* instead of *say* and *go*?

And finally ... reporting verbs

Recently, I had a debate with an editor about which words could be included in a grammar section on reporting verbs.

We were told that the following were decidedly **not** reporting verbs: *decide, intend, avoid, miss,* and *carry on.*

In one way, I agree: these are not part of the normal list of verbs included in the reporting verbs section of a coursebook. However, when you start thinking about it, trying to establish a clear difference between what **is** a reporting verb and what **isn't** seems pretty arbitrary. How do we know, for example, that *She's decided not to come to the wedding after all*? Couldn't the sentence be a report of a whole conversation we've had with her? How is *refused* – as in *She refused to come the wedding* – a reporting verb while *decide* is somehow not? You could argue that *avoid* on its own isn't reporting, but what about *He avoided the question*?

This brings us back to the point that reporting is an all-pervasive thing. The grammar element of reporting verbs, the patterns that follows them, is no different to understanding that there are different patterns that follow 'non-reporting' verbs. I don't see that creating a distinction about any of these things really helps students. As for the teaching of verb patterns themselves, well … Grrrr! That will be a bit of grammar nonsense for another day.

3

THE USE OF THE WORD 'GRAMMAR'

THE OTHER DAY, I opened my inbox and found an email encouraging me to celebrate March the 4th – 'World Grammar Day'. At first, I thought it was some kind of joke. Here we are, with the world going slightly mad, and what is the thing we most need to focus on? More grammar!

Because the conflict and disaster we see on the news every day is basically down to people who don't know the difference between a preposition and an adverb, right?! Or was this some peculiar revenge for our recent posts on grammar nonsense?

I looked further and it turned out the email was from Pearson, so the whole thing must be true! They can't just have made up this idea of World Grammar Day, can they? A little further investigation led me to Martha Brockenbrough, founder of the Society for the Promotion of Good Grammar (and a useful grammar book – available from all good book stores), who apparently established National Grammar Day in the US in 2008. So rather than being World Grammar Day, it seems it's actually American and British Grammar Day… and really it is more like 'Sell My Grammar Books Day'!

Is that grammar?

Now, in fact, it's not the commercial side of this which is annoying – we're definitely residing in a glass house there! No, what I find nonsensical here is the use of the word 'grammar' itself. When I looked at the Society for the Promotion of Good Grammar's blog – somewhat grandly called 'an online journal' – its most recent posts referred to:

- the misuse of *distinguished* when you should be using *extinguished*;
- a novel 'we' have written;
- the use of apostrophes and various spelling errors.

Look at other similar 'grammar' guides and you get things like the difference between *reticent* and *reluctant* or *hone in* and *home in*. All of which does force you to ask how on earth any of this is actually **grammar**! It seems deeply ironic that these people are telling us to be more precise with language and yet they repeatedly misuse, or generalise, the very word they believe to be so important and so precise – grammar!

Flexibility of meaning

If they were being more precise they should probably say instead something like:

- 'A lot of people have too narrow a vocabulary '
- 'They don't know enough language'
- 'They don't know how to use some words'
- 'They should use language more like me'
- 'Why didn't they do an English degree?'
- 'Basically, these people are a bit thick! Aren't they funny!'

However, I can accept that 'Their grammar is terrible' covers all of these bases and that there are plenty of other words and statements which are similarly imprecise / flexible – such as most grammar rules! I also believe the word 'grammar' is used in a similar generalised ways in other languages, so when a student says '*My* grammar is terrible', they actually mean 'I don't know enough language, I should use language more like you' (the teacher), etc.

The unfortunate shift from general use to precise use

So while we must accept that people will use 'grammar' in this general way as a synonym for 'language', as teachers, we have to understand that this is what it is happening and NOT misinterpret students' requests for 'more grammar' as being a *precise* use of the word, or as meaning that the student wants / needs more ELT grammar lessons, extra exercises from My Grammar Lab or Raymond Murphy-like pages, or even more and longer grammar explanations.

Instead, we'd do well to bear in mind what the great Michael Swan says: that there's no need to always adopt the same approach to grammar:

> the role of 'grammar' in language courses is often discussed as if 'grammar' were one homogeneous kind of thing. In fact, 'grammar' is an umbrella term for a large number of separate or loosely related language systems, which are so varied in nature that it is pointless to talk as if they should all be approached in the same way. How we integrate the teaching of structure and meaning will depend to a great extent on the particular language items involved. (Swan, 1985 p 80 link).

For example, we could deal with grammar more regularly through the way we tackle vocabulary and by giving longer and better examples to show how words are used – rather than relying on lists of single words.

Can things ever change?

In response to the post on Reported Speech, Michael McCarthy tweeted that he had written a similar debunking in 1998, and yet twenty years later it still features in coursebooks! Given this, you do have to ask: How can we actually change things?

Perhaps teachers could talk directly to publishers, examining bodies, and policy makers about crazy grammar rules that are perpetuated through books and through exams. I know that publishers often refer to the need to 'cover' grammar such as reported speech, but maybe they wouldn't if more teachers who don't like this kind of grammar nonsense complained to them about it.

If you are a trainer, make sure you tell your trainees it's nonsense and suggest they skip it in the book. Maybe we should write to examiners like Cambridge and ask for, say, reported speech to be removed as a tested component from their exams. We could also speak out about these issues more.

Basically, we need to be speaking more about **language** full stop at conferences and CPD days.

And as an antidote to 'World Grammar Day' and what it represents, perhaps we could also promote more blogs and blog posts undermining the 'grammar lords', such as Jena Barchas Lichtenstein's post supporting the use of 'fillers' – or maybe use Professor McCarthy's *Grammar of English* as a reference – or share vocabulary-based blogs like our Word/Chunk of the day posts on lexicallab.com!

4

STATIVE VERBS

Exceptions – it's not you, it's me

A LOT of grammar nonsense comes from the labels that we use and that we assume are sufficient explanation in themselves to generate their own correct examples. But when students attempt to produce examples in accordance with these labels, they discover these examples sound 'strange' to a teacher, so they will then often start asking why their examples <u>fail</u> to fit the labels.

Teachers can respond in one of three ways: there's the easy (woolly liberal) 'Oh, that's an exception', the more dogmatic 'It's just wrong/bad English', or there's the extended 'subtle' explanation that tries to encompass these more complex uses.

Of these three options, our preference would be 'the exception', because at least this is less likely to bring about feelings of failure in students. Exceptions are down to the idiosyncracies / curiosities / stupidities of the English language (delete as appropriate). They're essentially linguistic versions of the 'it's-not-you-it's-me' break-up line, which may be annoying and disappointing, but at least isn't laying the blame at your uselessness in the way that any 'it's bad English' response is. Nor will it bore you to death and ultimately confuse students like the extended explanation almost always does.

Usage above meaning

However, it may be the case that sometimes we'd be better off just avoiding the labels in the first place. Students need to accept ambiguity to be successful in language learning (and perhaps in life!). I think a key element of a lexical view of language is recognising that the meanings we give to any pieces of vocabulary or grammar can only ever be partial – and rather than giving more explanation, more 'meaning', more labels, we would be better off simply giving more examples of usage (and getting students to read and listen more to language in use).

The case of stative verbs

Take stative verbs. For those of you not familiar with this particular description, 'stative' is a label that tends to be given to a group of verbs that (supposedly) don't get used in the present continuous tense. So here are a few explanations from coursebooks (which shall remain nameless):

1. *Some verbs express a state – not an activity – and are usually used in the present simple only. For example: like, know, think, agree, understand, love.*
2. *We cannot normally use some verbs (stative verbs) in the continuous form. For example: agree, belong, cost, know, like, love, matter, mean, need, seem, understand, want.*
3. *We don't use stative verbs (be, have, like, love, hate, want) in the present continuous.*

Of course, as you may well be aware, many of these verbs **can** actually be used (and **are** used!) in the continuous form. *I'm loving it* has become incredibly widespread, perhaps thanks to the McDonald's slogan, but then the slogan no doubt came from advertisers picking up on usage. Here are some other common examples:

- *So if I'm understanding this right …*
- *It's costing me an arm and a leg!*
- *I've been meaning / wanting… to do it for ages*
- *I'm thinking of … leaving.*
- *He's having … a crisis of confidence.*
- *Ignore me, I'm just being silly.*
- *I was actually agreeing with you – I'm sorry if that didn't come across!*

So what is a stative verb? The problem of circularity

Part of the problem with using the term 'stative verbs' or 'verbs that express a state' is that it suggests the verbs are somehow infused with this sense all the time. In fact, at best we can say that some verbs *when they express the meaning of a state* are not usually expressed with a continuous form. But even then, does the example of *cost* above contradict that? Or is it not a state here? Which brings us to the rather bigger problem of what the hell a 'state' is anyway?

Think about your social media status: job, relationship, friends, likes, etc. Certainly, we would normally only say the following in the present simple:

- *I'm unemployed.*
- *I have a girlfriend.*
- *I hate my brother.*
- *I love swimming.*

But the following could also be expressions of these same 'states':

- *I'm not working.*
- *I'm seeing someone.*
- *I'm not speaking to my brother ever again.*
- *I'm really loving my swimming.*

So why are these verbs not seen as stative? Because they are used in the continuous form which is a mark of being non-stative! And so we enter a rather circular and pointless version of grammar rules – rather than a generative one. We don't use stative verbs with the present continuous because stative verbs are verbs which aren't used in the present continuous!

Do we actually need a new rule?

Interestingly, one of the grammar explanations quoted above, also gives the following example as an example which is *different* to the explanation about stative verbs:

- *Frazer **comes** from Scotland NOT ~~Frazer is coming from Scotland~~.*

The first thing to say about this is that the example is clearly <u>not</u> wrong if seen in terms of the verb *come* (there is no further explanation of why it's wrong). The first sentence explains the permanent fact of his birthplace/nationality; the second could be telling us where he is travelling from.

Come therefore can be used to express a 'state', but I've never seen it listed as a stative verb! Why not? Essentially, it's because the way *come* is used here is in keeping with the normal meanings that we attach to the present simple and the present continuous. However, isn't the same true of other 'stative' verbs?

Rather like we discussed with reported speech, we seem to have actually created a new category of rule where none is needed. If we take the idea that the present simple expresses ideas about now that we consider permanent or complete, or facts about ourselves, compared to continuous forms which are essentially temporary and unfinished or in progress, then both the 'stative' and the continuous use of all the verbs so far mentioned fit these meanings more or less without creating any new categories for students to worry about.

Present simple for present and complete actions/states

I think part of the issue here is also that we forget the 'present and complete' use of the present simple in football commentary, like 'He takes on Stones . . . He shoots ... He scores'. Neither the past simple nor the present continuous fit here when commentating on events you are watching and *the same is true* when we say things like *I know / I understand / I agree.* They happen at this moment, but we see them as <u>complete</u> in the moment.

It won't solve everything, but maybe it's one less problem!

This is not to say, of course, that our meanings for the present simple and present continuous are unambiguous and will never lead to student 'errors'. However, we would suggest that more explanation and extended lists of meanings will not actually help. In the end, usage that corresponds with what the vast majority of fluent speakers say can only come from learners experiencing the language of the vast majority of people! In terms of study and learning, students are also probably better off trying to expand the meanings they are able to make in English through learning more vocabulary.

5

RELATIVE CLAUSES

THIS IS LESS a post about the craziness of description and more one about the way in which grammar is presented and the expectation that grammar should always be practised – and practised in particular ways.

Grammar McNuggets and overprotectiveness

Scott Thornbury has criticised coursebooks (and related teaching) for providing what he calls Grammar McNuggets (https://scottthornbury.wordpress.com/2010/09/18/g-is-for-grammar-mcnuggets/). The comparison is with the McDonald's chicken, where the meat is removed of skin and detached from the bone, chopped up, and processed so that it no longer looks in any way like a chicken and can be served up in a bite-sized chunk without any mess.

Likewise, grammar gets removed from its context or natural environment and is processed in order to illustrate a particular 'rule'. I can assure you that when writing material, examples definitely do get removed from exercises because they seem to break rules even though they are perfectly natural, while rather unnatural sentences (ones you couldn't imagine saying) are created to ensure 'rule fit' and single answers.

Sometimes these changes are requested by editors. Often, they come about because we, the writers, self-censor what we produce – partly because we know what editors will say, but also (importantly) because we can imagine what students might say / ask in class. We then think of the inexperienced teacher who might not be able to give an answer and, as a result, may end up tongue-tied and looking foolish. We are probably being overprotective and perhaps we should allow more ambiguity. Could we actually simplify our explanations more, as we suggested with our post on stative verbs? Could we sometimes just give examples and no explanation?

Supersize me

Grammar McNuggets is a lovely term that encapsulates what is often wrong with grammar materials and teaching. However, I think one slight problem with the term is that it can also suggest that there is something wrong with small manageable-sized bits of teaching and learning. A McNugget as an individual bit of food is not terribly harmful and could be a tasty bite-sized snack. What's of more concern is when the McNugget is not only the main-stay of your diet, but you also supersize!

How is that reflected in grammar teaching? Well, the first issue is the demand to present and practise grammar in the same kinds of ways – often very artificially. The second – bigger – issue is that as your level increases, it appears that the grammar sections in classroom material must also increase or else be more densely packed. Publishers, editors and, dare I say it, some teachers state that you must 'increase the challenge' for advanced learners – which seems to mean some kind of man versus food challenge: you can't eat one small portion of fresh, organic chicken nuggets, you must eat a whole barrelful of the processed stuff with an added pint of a sweet sugary sauce (for the sauce, read: the 'fun' communicative activity!).

Supersizing relative clauses

Take relative clauses. We start off by presenting *that* and *who* (often first seen at Pre-Intermediate, which seems ridiculously late). We then have *that, who, which, where, when, why* at Intermediate. Next, we have all of these and insist on forcing students to distinguish between defining and non-defining clauses. Then we have all these things **again**, with *whom* and the position prepositions added in; and then we have to include 'reduced relative clauses' . . . and so it goes on until the Advanced student either has to deal with two or three pages of grammar notes or all these elements get crammed into one extremely highly processed and standardised page.

Seriously, can anyone take such an amount of information in and then apply it? No! But don't let that stop us from doing it anyway – and then devising some convoluted way to practise it.

Non-defining v. defining relative clauses – Grrrr . . .

A particular point of annoyance here is the contrasting of defining / non-defining relative clauses. Mea culpa, for I have written exercises on this as it is 'what the market expects!' However, increasingly, I do find myself wondering why so much is made of the difference. And when is *not* knowing the difference ever a problem? Take this example from an old edition of a well-known coursebook. Students have to say which is more likely to fill the gap – a defining or non-defining clause. For example:

- *The apple tree at the end of our garden___ ___ needs to be chopped down.*
- *People ___ ___ live longer.*
- *She married a man ___ .*
- *Let me introduce you to Peter James ___ .*
- *Jane's the sort of person ___ ___ .*

As a way of showing the difference, I think it's actually rather clever. I like it. However, I then think why would someone ONLY say *'She married a man'* or *'She's the sort of person'*? Clearly, they wouldn't, so why even have this in the task? I mean, what's it really adding? Why not just have the non-defining gaps to show how that can be done and then get suggestions on how to fill them? The reason would be: because it's too easy, and heaven forbid that we make language learning easier! We need challenge! Eating Chicken McNuggets is too convenient – you need to eat them using a spoon held between your toes!

As if to reiterate the pointlessness of making this distinction, look at that first 'non-defining' relative clause. Here's what the exercise then goes on to add:

The apple tree at the end of our garden, which my grandfather planted 70 years ago, needs to be chopped down.

But, of course, this sentence could equally be arranged as a defining relative clause with no difference in meaning!

> *The apple tree which my grandfather planted 70 years ago at the end of our garden needs to be chopped down.*

And then you have to ask what actually **is** this sentence? Something you'd write? Or say? If the ideas were part of a conversation, surely it's more likely it would be something like this:

> *A: Is that an apple tree at the end of the garden?*
> *B: Yeah – unfortunately it's got a disease – we need to cut it down.*
> *B: What a shame.*
> *A: It is. My grandfather actually planted that 70 years ago.*
> *B: Oh no! Can't you save it? …*

In other words – with no @*#! relative clauses at all!

Basically, these types of embedded non-defining relative clauses are fairly uncommon in conversation (though there are other types that we'll look at in the next chapter). And even if they were common, they wouldn't obviously be any different to a defining relative clause because there would be no commas. Ah, but there is phonology! There's that subtle change in pace and tone, isn't there? And so we have students trying to listen and distinguish between the following and say how many daughters the person has:

- *My daughter, who lives in Paris, has a dog.*
- *My daughter who lives in Paris has a dog.*

But what kind of mad person really talks like this? When someone is talking about their daughter having a dog (for example), who would casually throw into the middle of that statement that she, say, lives in Paris? Answers to us on a post card of the Eiffel Tower (or, failing that, via email)! Why do we do this? Because we must differentiate and challenge ... and because we must practise!

Standardised communicative practice

Practice generally has to be of two kinds – one where the form / structure is manipulated in some way or is discussed, and secondly, one where it is practised 'communicatively' whilst at the same time allowing plenty of opportunities for students to generate new sentences using the grammar.

In and of themselves, I don't mind either of these things: there seems to be good evidence that drawing attention to a structure / form / pattern helps students on the journey towards uptake – even if, as some argue, this is merely speeding up the journey, rather than changing the route. I think trying to use new language and to integrate it with what you know already is also a fundamental part of learning.

However, not all grammar lends itself to a sustained communicative production, which is why either unnatural contexts, conversations, and tasks are created to squeeze them in, or we fall back on what have become almost standards. Step forward, defining words and the general knowledge quiz:

- What do you call a person *who* writes these grammar practice tasks yet complains about it in his blog? (A hypocrite)
- What's the name of the book *that* he wrote? (*Outcomes Pre-intermediate* – Unit 14)!

In my defence, I would say neither defining words nor quizzes are especially bad ways to practise English. I mean, defining is at least something students might do to ask someone for a word in English (even if Google might be more successful!). However, as a teacher and learner, I think relative clauses are so much more than this. They are so useful, so varied, and so ubiquitous that reducing them to this kind of practice and one focus in five coursebook levels is actually really underplaying their value.

Grammar olives

I think most grammar teaching could be reduced to smaller, more regular bits integrated with vocabulary, but I'm beginning to think this is particularly true of grammar such as relative clauses. This kind of teaching might come through correction / improvement of students' English after some genuine communication. At other times, we might give mini-presentations of typical relative clause chunks with limited examples of how they can be changed to help do a specific task. I see this as something packaged and 'snacky', but at the same time closer to nature – a grammar olive, perhaps, or a grammar orange segment, if you prefer something sweeter!

Next up, it's time for some more grammar curiosities. It can't all be misery and frustration! We'll be looking at some of those grammar olives for relative clauses.

6

RELATIVE CLAUSES – SOME CURIOSITIES

Too much choice

WHEN WE ORIGINALLY PUBLISHED THE post on relative clauses that we saw in the last chapter, we asked if anyone had any good ideas about contexts for presenting and practising them. There was a deafening silence! Perhaps this is like when you tell someone you speak a foreign language and the other person says *Go on! Say something*. You're left speechless, paralysed by the infinite choice of what you could say. Essentially, relative clauses could come up in all kinds of situations, so thinking of one particular context maybe left people similarly nonplussed. Or maybe they weren't nonplussed — maybe it was the guilty silence of teachers who hate teaching relative clauses and so have been avoiding it for years!

Do we need to teach them at all?

Well, feel guilt no more, because I'm going to suggest that not doing a lesson on them is a good idea! Instead, we could simply draw attention to them as and when they come up. When I was at IATEFL Glasgow a few years ago, this was also suggested by Danny Norrington-Davies, who I think was quoting Martin Parrot. I've recently found myself looking more at Parrot's book, *Grammar for English Language Teachers*, and finding many words of wisdom.

Certainly, in Romance languages, there isn't anything really syntactically different about a relative clause – they basically come in the same part of the sentence. What about in other languages? I would be very interested to learn. We could see relative clauses as primarily a question of learning the words *which, who, that, where* etc. – or to put it a better way, the English equivalents of the relative pronouns in the foreign language.

I believe in some languages, a relative pronoun for a defining clause might be different to a non-defining one. Students need to know that equivalent in English, but not how a relative clause works – they know that already. OK, so in English, we often leave out the relative pronoun, but you don't have to. This eliding of the pronoun might be something we could deal with receptively and wait for students to develop that style (or not develop it, if they so wish in the world of English as a Lingua Franca!).

Some grammar olives for relative clauses

One way awareness can be drawn to relative clauses is through two-way translation. You might have an example such as *This is the guy I was telling you about*, which could be useful when introducing someone. Ask the students to translate it into their own language. Then they can cover the original and translate it back into English and comment on any differences they notice. This could be done with single sentences as they arise for example when a student was searching to use a relative clause or used one wrongly (a two-minute activity). You might also provide additional examples to illustrate the pattern – something we did in the first edition of the **Outcomes** series – and get students to translate all of them to see how the sentence is patterned and generative.

- *That's the place I was telling you about yesterday.*
- *She's the woman I was talking to earlier.*
- *Did you see I sent you that article I was telling you about?*

Thoughts on the controlled practice and free practice in PPP

What's interesting to me here is that while all these sentences have the same function, you would be quite unlikely to say them all within the same context or conversation. When it comes to communicative practice, it is, therefore, quite hard to have a sensible context which provides multiple opportunities for using relative clauses.

My view is that we should probably just accept this. The translation activity is a kind of controlled practice (why should the second P in Present Practice and Produce be a long activity?), and we could have a short free conversation practice perhaps based on any one of these sentences. So what if students don't use any other relative clauses in their conversation? They'll be practising plenty of other grammar in this freer Production stage as well. That's worthwhile, isn't it?

Having said that, we may be able to provide groups of relative clauses which allow students more choice and several opportunities to use them within an extended speaking. For example:

- *That's exactly what I was saying earlier.*
- *That's not what I meant to say.*
- *That's the point I was trying to make.*
- *That's the word I wanted, not X.*
- *That's who I meant to say, not Y!*

Relative clauses, common modifiers, and chunks

These previous examples could, of course, simply be taught as useful chunks of language without reference to the grammar at all. A narrow view of a lexical approach would say that is exactly what you should do – reference to grammar is to be avoided.

However, as we have made clear in previous posts, this is certainly not how we view lexical teaching. Instead what we are trying to do is work with collocation and useful chunks within grammar teaching.

This is something which Bruno Leys presented in another talk at IATEFL. His exercises look at relative clauses as a kind of collocation. I think there is definitely something in this – especially when we broaden the concept of relative clauses to general post-modification of nouns, including prepositional phrases and participle phrases. So, for example, we might have these common collocations:

- *the car in front*
- *the car coming in the opposite direction*
- *the car parked next to me*
- *the car I had before*

Apart from the two-way translation, you could put these in a simple gap-fill that emphasises the grammar element. In each case, we could ask 'which car?' to draw attention to the grammar function:

- *As I was backing out, I caught the side of the car___ . I left quite a bad scratch.*
- *I find this is a lot cheaper to run than the car___ . That one used to guzzle fuel.*
- *Apparently, they were trying to overtake a truck and they collided with a car ___ .*
- *The car ___ braked really suddenly, and I almost went into the back of it.*

A context of talking about cars and driving incidents might allow a practice of these. However, note that when planning such a task, vocabulary is likely to be far more of a problem than the grammar! We could do a number of these sentences where we first process the grammar, but we then would need to go back and look at the vocabulary and ask questions about it to check and develop students' understanding. Again, this is a central idea of lexical teaching – exercises can serve twin functions. They are not separated out. Grammar and vocab work together, so why not develop exercises that recognise that fact?

While the above example can work for, say, a B2 level or higher, we could still do the same kind of thing at lower levels. For example, when looking at conversations about deciding where to eat, we could give students these chunks and patterns:

- *the bar next door*
- *the cafe down the road*
- *that X place with the terrace on Y Rd*
- *the place we went to last week*
- *a new place in Z a friend was telling me about*

We could perhaps brainstorm other examples in class based on the location of the class and the students in the room. We could then provide other frames to go with these noun phrases:

- *The ___ is nice.*
- *The ___ does sandwiches.*
- *The ___ is OK for something quick.*
- *How about the ___? We haven't been there for a while.*
- *How about the ___? They do a nice lunch menu.*
- *How about the ___? We could sit outside.*
- *There's ___. They said it's great / It's supposed to be great.*

If you really wanted to simplify this, you could stick to the prepositional phrases. It is strange, I think, that while prepositions and prepositional phrases are a common part of low-level courses, as in *There's a pub on Upper Street*, materials rarely follow this up by showing students how these same prepositional phrases can be used to define nouns in other sentences:

- *I never go to the bar round the corner.*
- *They've closed the bar next to the station.*

I don't see why such noun phrases could not be taught to an Elementary student. There is nothing conceptually complicated about them – or linguistically complex (assuming they have been taught the prepositional phrases already). Again, we might not expect immediate take up, and we can imagine errors, but it may speed up the journey.

Some more collocations

Of course, these defining relative clauses will often follow very common nouns: *man, woman, people, place, thing, stuff, way, shop, bar, hotel,* etc. Perhaps, and I have never tried this in class, it would be interesting at low levels (A1-B1) to give noun phrases based on these words and ask students to generate sentences or stories about them; and / or we could add other common phrases to modify the noun:

- *the woman... standing in front of me in the queue / sitting next to me / behind me / I met / I was telling you about*
- *people... waiting / hanging around / protesting / I work with / in my class / next door*
- *the way... home / to work / there / to the airport / out*

- *place… nearby / we stayed in / we went to / you live in / you're moving to*

The 'human' examples above include 'reduced' relative clauses – which are not usually taught in coursebooks until Upper Intermediate / B2 level. However, do students actually have to think of them as reduced relative clauses at all in these cases to make use of them – and perhaps even generate their own patterns? I don't think so.

Are -ing clauses reduced relative clauses anyway?

Another example where using an *-ing* form to define a noun could be taught is through the pattern *there is / there are X -ing*. We learn *there is / there are* at an elementary level. We might follow this up with *there was / there were* – maybe – but I have rarely seen it taught in coursebooks as a thing at lower levels. But again, is it such a difficult further step? And wouldn't learning it help develop an awareness and uptake of the 'reduced relative clause' pattern in other contexts?

I do have a question here, though, when considering these as a reduction of a full relative clause, as opposed to an *-ing* form modifying the noun it follows.

It seems clear that *There were lots of people already queuing when I got there* IS 'reduced' from *'lots of people who were already queuing'*, but what about *'There was a problem finding accommodation?'* What's the relative clause that is being 'reduced' there? And in either case, is this what speakers are really doing – reducing relative clauses? Do speakers *start* by thinking of the relative clause and then choose to reduce it? Seems unlikely to me.

. . . which was nice.

And finally, a thought on the non-defining relative clauses in speech. We mentioned before that they are not very common. However, we do quite often use ones which basically modify a previous clause; in other words, we use them to comment on what has just been said. The '…which was nice' chunk actually became a catchphrase in the BBC sketch show, *The Fast Show*. The character would list a series of incredible happenings in their life, which would then be followed, with typically English understatement, by the catchphrase. We could provide examples for two-way translation as suggested above:

- *The airline bumped us up to business class, which was very nice.*
- *I left my ID at home and had to go back, which was a bit of a pain.*
- *They got married in Littlehampton, which is where they first met.*
- *I'd told him hundreds of times before not to do it, which is why I was so pissed off.*

Alternatively, as a practice you could work either by giving the relative clause and getting students to think of the rest of the sentence, or you could give sentences and get students to think of the relative clauses:

- ___ , *which was nice.*
- *I left my ID at home and had to go back, ___ .*

In either case, they could see how many different ideas they could come up with in a *Fast Show* style, and you might even find that students produced similar comic effects! Working with common chunks doesn't mean we can't be creative and playful at times.

7

INDIRECT QUESTIONS

I CAN'T QUITE DECIDE if the EFL view of indirect questions is pure foolishness or more a question of a missed
opportunity. I guess I probably think it's more the latter,
but when you start thinking about these things, it's diffi-

cult not to see the absurdity of what we say. So, first the nonsense — or the half-truths, if we want to be charitable.

What we tell students about indirect questions

Coursebook 1: *Indirect questions use the same order as the positive and there is no* do / does / did. *We often make direct questions into indirect to make them sound 'softer' or more polite.*

Coursebook 2: *Indirect questions are more polite than direct questions. You often use them when you talk to strangers or people you don't know well. You tend to begin a conversation with indirect questions then continue with direct questions* [This is followed by a table showing the transformations from direct to indirect questions and missing *do / does / did*, etc.].

Grammar book: *Indirect questions have a different word order from direct question and no question marks. We don't use* do *in indirect questions. With indirect yes / no questions, we use* if *or* whether. *They mean the same.*

Forgetting that there is a direct question before an 'indirect' question

Now, I can almost hear you say what exactly is wrong with that, then! Hey, I can almost hear **myself** saying it! But then I ask myself 'What do you mean by *indirect questions have a different order and don't use* do / did, *etc.*'' and look at some actual examples of real English!

- *Do you know what time it is?*
- *Did you ask when we'll get the results?*
- *Do you remember where I put it?*
- *Do you think you could possibly give me a hand?*
- *Does she know who you are?*

Don't **all** these 'indirect questions' actually contain *do, does,* or *did*? Don't they also have the normal word order of questions?! Oh, Andrew, now you're just being obstreperous, as my mother used to say. The *Do you know* is not really the question, it's the *what time*, the *when* etc. **That's** the indirect question.

I would suggest that this message is a bit of a problem. It comes across as if we're saying that the *Do you know* bit is not actually important or not really a question in itself. We are basically just asking a normal question, and for the sake of politeness, we add these starters, which have the inconvenient effect of changing the word order of the question you really want to ask.

This seems a slightly perverse way of viewing things. It's what I might call **the transformation fallacy**, which have also seen in reported speech: the idea that when we speak, we take a 'base' form and make a transformation in our minds to create a new meaning, when in actual fact what we do (I think) is go directly for whatever form we want because that's the meaning we actually want to convey.

In this case, that means what we want to ask **first** is *Do you know, Did you ask, Do you think, Do you mind,* etc. That's important not only in terms of reducing confusion for students about the use of auxiliaries and question order, but also in terms of thinking about why we use 'indirect questions'.

Did you know we ask indirect questions to be polite? Really?

Seen from this point of view, there's nothing really to learn about when we use indirect questions other than under-standing the meanings of the words *know, ask, think, mind, remember,* etc. As with all other verbs, when we ask a question with these words, the meaning *doesn't change*: we want to know if a person knows, thinks, minds, remembers, etc. It's NOTHING directly to do with politeness or making things softer. That is simply connected to the particular verb used (e.g. *mind*).

I don't ask the person in the street D*o you know what the time is* as opposed to W*hat's the time* in order to be polite! I ask because I don't know if they know and I want to show them that I don't necessarily expect them to have an answer. In fact, if I see they have a watch, and I want to be polite, I'm just as likely to ask directly *Could you tell me the time?* – and that wouldn't be seen as odd or impolite.

In terms of politeness, *Could you* is perfectly sufficient, *unless* we believe we are putting someone out and that the person may well **not** be able to do something (*Do you think you could give me a lift to the station?*). In fact, using an 'indirect question' could also be seen as sarcastic and rude: *We all know you like the sound of your own voice, but do you think you could possibly give someone else a chance to speak?*

Does she know who you are? No, sadly.

There are, of course, millions of instances where we ask 'indirect' questions that very clearly have nothing to do with politeness. The question above is a good (though personally difficult) example of this. I have been asked quite a few times *Does she know who you are?* because my mother has dementia. This is not a genuine question about me (*Who are you?*) made indirect for politeness. It is simply a question to get a fact – a yes / no question, actually, which does not use *if* or *whether*!

Are you sure you need *if* or *whether* for an indirect yes/no question?

Furthermore, that rule 'With indirect yes / no questions, we use *if* or *whether*' actually depends on the verb you are using. *Could you open the door for me?* is a yes / no question. However, the 'indirect' *'Do you think you could open the door for me?* cannot use *if* / *whether*. The same would be true of *I reckon / do you reckon, I guess, I suppose,* and various other verbs. And this is the key thing, I think. Really, the grammar we are focusing on here is **verbs that are typi-**

cally followed by a clause and the words that link those verbs and the clause. The way the verb and clause link depends on the verb you are using.

The real grammar: verbs followed by a clause

Sometimes we say the verb is followed by a 'that' clause and a dictionary such as Macmillan often shows the entry as 'think (that)'. However, it's far more common not to use any word to link with the clause. Have a 'google fight' with these pairs of sentences: put each example into a search engine with quotation marks around them and see how many hits they get. You will find that the first sentence in each pair wins hands down.

- *Do you think he's lying? / Do you think that he's lying?*
- *I think she knows. / I think that she knows.*

Obviously, there are many verbs with a similar pattern – *remember, forget, say, claim, admit,* etc. – and the results are likely to be similar when you compare the frequency of sentences with and without 'that'.

With some verbs such as *know, wonder, remember, etc.,* you can link with a question word / phrase such as *where, what time, how long,* etc., or *if / whether.*

- *Do you know how much it'll cost?*
- *Did you ask if they could give us lift?*

- *I wonder where he is now.*
- *I've already forgotten what he taught me.*
- *I don't know how much more I can take.*
- *I'm not sure if I can come yet.*

Some of these are questions, of course, and some of these are not, but when they are created as questions, the patterns after the verb are the same – obviously. The question formation of the verb itself also follows the normal rule of questions, as I said at the beginning.

A solution disconnected from the problem is no solution at all

So why all the fuss? Apart from the possible transformation fallacy mentioned earlier, it probably comes about because students do sometimes use question inversion after these verbs. In response to that, teachers notice the error. They correct it and then start teaching about it, perhaps in an effort to prevent it from happening again.

Then writers start including it in their coursebooks, but to do so it needs to be presented as **a thing** – indirect questions – and so now we have to treat it like other bits of grammar – as having a particular form and function – and we lose sight of the underlying grammar. Is that really a good idea? You will gather from this post that I don't think it is. It seems to me that it brings a certain amount of confusion for very little gain.

Showing the bigger picture – moving beyond indirect questions

However – and this is the missed opportunity – it also seems to me that we are failing to teach these **verb patterns** fully and consistently. While we teach about verbs followed by -*ing* or infinitives at quite an early stage (*like doing / want to do*), I don't recall seeing much focus on verb + clause – maybe because 'clause' is a bit more technical than –*ing* or infinitive. Yet verbs with these patterns are some of the most common in English, and we could easily show patterns without using any jargon: for example, through exemplification tables, translation, and students trying to generate their own questions and sentences.

Understanding the shared patterns of these verbs might also help avoid spending time banging on not just about indirect questions as some oddly separate piece of grammar, but also the supposed 'rules' of questions in reported speech. It's curious that *Did you ask* or *did they say* rarely feature as stems in indirect question exercises, maybe because they appear to be reporting rather than being indirect questions to be polite. Yet the verb pattern grammar is *the same.*

Finally, I should say, that thinking about this issue recently and looking at various coursebooks and grammars, one did stand out – and it was Martin Parrot's *Grammar for English Language Teachers*. While he uses the term *noun-clause*, which I personally don't find the best description, in all other ways he does much to clarify my vaguer thoughts on the matter, and I once again doff my hat to his clarity and good sense.

8

FUTURE FORMS

"IT IS a truth universally acknowledged that EFL students attending a class must be in want of a good grammar explanation. However little known the feelings or views of such students may be on their first entering a classroom, this truth is so well fixed in the minds of the ELT profession, it is considered as the right of all teachers to spend time spouting nonsense about grammar."

So said Jane Austen – well, almost!

With this our next chapter on grammar nonsense, we come to **futures**. Perhaps a truth somewhat less universally acknowledged – in coursebooks, at any rate – is that the structures used to refer to the future are by no means clearly defined. 'Mistakes' connected with the use of, say, *will* instead of *be going to* or the present continuous would rarely be seen by a native speaker (or any other fluent user, for that matter) as a mistake based on a concept of meaning. In other words, the listener would in no way be confused as to the intended meaning. Instead, they might just feel that the utterance sounded a little bit odd – and often they wouldn't even think that.

Bearing this in mind, we should take a step back for a moment and just think about what we tell our students about the meanings of different future structures. Usually, it's things like this:

- It's an arrangement.
- It's planned.
- It's an intention.
- It's a prediction based on present (or past!) evidence.
- It's a timetabled event.
- It's a prediction.

I could go on, but you get the idea. We are so familiar with these explanations that we often fail to stop and think about how anyone can possibly tell the difference between these things! Arrangements are clearly planned, or intended, as are timetables! And what prediction is NOT based on some kind of present evidence?

I think the sun is going to shatter into a million pieces and fall like sparkly buttercups.

We can pretty categorically say that the above is **not** a prediction based on any evidence; but then again, if you were to hear me come up with such a claim in conversation, you would think I was a crazy person and take a long walk around me – or else admire the fact I possessed the imagination of a five-year-old! Oh, and if you've been severely affected by the kind of nonsense routinely peddled by EFL material, you might also notice that I used *going to* there... when your books all say I should've used *will*. Lordy Lord!

Then, of course, there's the question of what the difference is between a plan, an arrangement, and an intention. In a very amusing clip from the show **The Trip**, Steve Coogan and Rob Brydon talk about the typical scene in a medieval costume drama before a battle:

> '… and they always say something like 'Gentlemen to bed, gentlemen to bed for **we leave** at first light. Tomorrow **we battle** and **we may lose** our lives, …'

They continue to play with this idea, and subsequently say:

> *Gentlemen, to bed! For we leave at nine thirty [...-ish].*

> *Gentlemen, to bed! For at daybreak I will … we will breakfast!*

> *Brother, tomorrow we shall have breakfast. We shall rise at 9, and we shall head off tomorrow morning …*

Surely, all these uses – simple present, *will*, *shall* – could be interchangeable. Now, of course they are speaking in a kind of mock old-fashioned way, but imagine if they were talking in a more modern style about getting a flight instead of having a fight. The meanings we give simply will not produce these sentences:

> A: *What time are you getting up?* (The present continuous? How can that be? Who did you arrange that with – the airline?)

> B: *6. It'll take an hour to get to the airport* (Is that a

prediction really? Based on what? Why not present simple? Or going to?) *and the flight's at 9.*

Now look at these sentences below. What are we supposed to say about the differences in grammar **that will make sense to a student**?

- *I'll be seeing him tomorrow, so I'll ask him.*
- *I'm going to see him tomorrow, so I'll ask him.*
- *I'll see him tomorrow, so I'll ask him.*
- *I'm seeing him tomorrow, so I'll ask him*
- *I see him tomorrow, so I'll ask him.*

In the sad, sorry days of my youth (and somewhat misguided by Michael Lewis's most overrated work, *Meaning and the English Verb*), I used to spend whole classes discussing the fictitious difference in meaning between such sentences, and I am ashamed to say I have been drawn into such things since as well . . . despite the fact that **they all basically mean the same thing**! These days, I think the only one I might – *might* – bother singling out for any special attention is the last one, where it may be assumed this is a weekly meeting I always have – maybe, possibly. But, actually, even then, would it make any difference to you as the listener? I think not.

While humans clearly do possess an innate capacity to see patterns and create meaning, in the end, we take what we hear and create that meaning internally for ourselves, and it is confirmed or adapted according to our successes or failures in communication. This is why, I think, meanings and usage shifts over time, and it's also why trying to impose meanings on areas of grammar such as this or correcting students on the basis of meaning is somewhat fruitless. Almost inevitably, what happens is that the same examples are used repeatedly (fess up: how many of you have reached for *I think I'm going to sneeze / be sick* when trying to explain away 'predictions based on present evidence'?), while other examples are crafted to match the meaning, resulting in some highly unlikely sentences.

One of my favourites is this gem: *The cars are going to crash!* I'd like to think that if I were in a situation where I needed this sentence and found I had time to say anything at all, my preference would be not to state the bleeding obvious, but rather to go for something more basic and Anglo-Saxon!

So what to do? I really don't think there's an easy answer here. My personal preference would be to present structures as they are used and pretty much only say 'This refers to the future' And taking such an approach, we should be free to give examples of all the different structures from a lower level when they are naturally needed or used. If students ask why one structure is used here and not another, perhaps we should simply return the question and focus on the context it is being used in. This is an approach recommended in an interesting book by Danny Norrington-Davies called *From Rules to Reasons*. Or maybe just tell them that it actually doesn't matter if they use will instead of going to, etc!

However, I do understand the pressure to give an explanation (from students, teachers, and publishers). If you do fall back on the traditional explanations, I think it's best to again focus on the reason structures are used in a **real example** and emphasize that these things are vague and that we can express the same idea in other ways too.

In general, I would like teachers to avoid exercises that ask students to differentiate meanings and would opt instead for texts with natural examples, where students might simply notice the different forms or be tested on how the form works.

Other than that, we could provide repeated opportunity for discussions or tasks that may generate a variety of future forms (something which most books don't do) – and fret less about an area that's really not worthy of your anxieties!

9

THE SYLLABUS FOR BEGINNERS

YOU MIGHT THINK that at Beginner level, as the grammar is rather basic, there surely can't be much in the way of nonsense to report on! Plurals do indeed generally end in *s*, adjectives are not modified with a plural *s* in English, and they usually go before a noun, rather than after it, etc. No controversy there, but writing **Outcomes Beginner** actually threw up quite a lot of nonsense for us to deal with – as well as the occasional curiosity – with the biggest issue being the 'Beginner syllabus' itself.

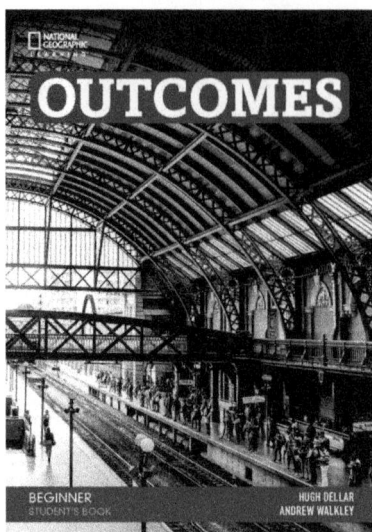

For those of you who are unaware of how the book-writing process works, preparation for most coursebooks starts with the construction of the syllabus. This generally involves making a list of the grammar and topics covered in other books at the same level! This selection is then seen as what needs to be covered and your USPs (your Unique Selling Points) – whether they be puppets or tasks or real-world texts or whatever – are fashioned around these "essentials".

At higher levels, what is deemed essential becomes less secure and so there is some flexibility to work around the core of items you find in all books. However, when it comes to Beginner books and, to a large degree, Elementary ones too, both the grammatical content AND the order are pretty much exactly the same in every series aimed at the global market.

Basically, it goes something like this:

Units 1-4

>   verb *be* + plurals / subject pronouns and possessives
>   / articles / *this, that, these, those* / adjectives

Units 5-8

>   present simple + adverbs of frequency / preposi-
>   tions of place and time

Unit 9-11

>   past simple – *be* followed by regular forms, which
>   are then followed by irregular forms

Unit 12

>   *can / can't* and/or *there is / there are* and/or *would like*

Unit 13 and 14

>   present continuous – present meaning and some-
>   times future meaning (or *be going to*)

OK, there is some *slight* variation in the second half of
books, once *be* and the present simple have been firmly
established. One or two books introduce the present

continuous (in its present meaning – started, but not finished) before the past simple. One or two books introduce *there is / are* earlier as part of the focus on *be*. There are also different lengths of units and of books themselves, but these have marginal impact on the above.

What's more important are the 'rules' that accompany this order:

1. The book shall not contain examples of a structure/ grammar before it is formally presented.
2. The book should try to restrict practice / output to the grammar that is presented.
3. 'Different' meanings of a form will be clearly separated – ambiguous examples should be avoided.

Essentially, they present a linear building block approach to learning: practise and 'master' one area before moving on to the next.

It's the combination of this fixed grammar syllabus and the set rules – as much as the actual order of the syllabus – that is, to my mind, grammar nonsense.

It's nonsense for these reasons:

- It restricts the communication that can take place in class and all too often leads to stupid / childish practice.
- It presents an unreal view of English by preventing some of the most frequent words and patterns in English (*been / should / will*, etc.) from even being **seen**.
- It assumes learning is linear and so restricts repeated exposure over time.
- It assumes students are in an English bubble of the coursebook and classroom – like the Internet and the mass media somehow don't exist.

But even if the building block approach were true, what strikes me as utterly bonkers is that **Elementary** courses then follow almost **the same** pattern (albeit slightly speeded up) and with the **same rules**. What's that all about?

Surely, if we have built the blocks correctly, then you could have examples of past simple, *be going to*, and other patterns from the very first page of Elementary, and we could introduce *been* or *will*, say, in unit two or three.

Instead, on average, Elementary students have to wait until around page 54 to see their next example of the word *went*, and you finally get to see *been* – one of the top hundred most common words in English – in unit 12. If you make it that far, that is! Isn't this really just an admission that something has gone wrong?

Beginner courses, it seems, are basically building Jenga-style towers. They are perhaps fun at times to create, but they have no long-term purpose – other than to collapse, so can we start again!

10

SHORT ANSWERS AND AUXILIARIES

FOLLOWING on from the previous post about the way the syllabus in most Beginner-level books is constructed, one of the areas that continues to dominate at this level – and which I find most annoying – is the teaching of auxiliaries in short answers. When coursebooks (and, no doubt, a lot of teachers), present yes / no questions in any new tense, students are taught to mirror this with *Yes / No* + subject + the same auxiliary (+not).

For example:

> A: *Do you work here?*
> B: *Yes, I do / No, I don't.*
> A: *Are you using this?*
> B: *Yes, I am. / No, I'm not.*
> A: *Have you seen him today?*
> B: *Yes, I have. / No, I haven't.*

Obviously, this grammar in itself is not nonsense, as we do use auxiliaries in this way – it's just that I have never understood why this is deemed essential at such low levels. Surely, when students have next to no English, we should be providing them with **the simplest** ways of fulfilling their communicative desires and making the most of the little language they have.

What does *I do* or *I don't* add to the communication here? Nothing. Students can sound perfectly correct just by saying *Yes* or *No*, and if they didn't have to practise using the auxiliaries, they could focus their attention on language which is more relevant to their immediate needs, such as other questions they could ask or the next part of the conversation, or some new words or … well, I'm sure you can also think of something more useful!

SHORT ANSWERS AND AUXILIARIES   71

There are additional problems with teaching short answer replies in this way. By teaching them as the default form (why else would we teach them?), the corollary is that NOT using them is either 'incorrect' or marked for rudeness or emphasis and, therefore, teachers are encouraged to spend additional time on 'correcting' their non-use and re-practising replying with auxiliaries.

In doing so, we end up misrepresenting how conversations in English really work. That's because, firstly, we don't follow this pattern this with all *yes / no* questions – particularly modals.

A: Shall I do it for you?
B: Yes, you shall!

Secondly, we frequently don't reply with the same auxiliary as in the question:

A: Are you going out later?
B: I might.

Having taught the mirroring rule, we may well find ourselves in the absurd position of then having to explain non-use or different uses. The reality is we have got things the wrong way round entirely!

The default way of answering *yes / no* questions is simply to use *yes / no*, following Grice's Maxims. In fact, the *Longman Grammar of Spoken and Written English* (see section 14.3.3.6) states that *Yeah* is actually the 'canonical' or default response, being far more common than *Yes*. As such, adding an auxiliary and / or using the 'full form' of *Yes* will actually mark our replies with emphasis or additional meaning (such as rudeness!).

From this point of view, we should probably leave the use of auxiliaries in short answers to acquisition – in other words, exposure to normal usage over time – which we might support through drawing attention to their use at Intermediate levels and above.

Which brings me to a final thought. Paradoxically, we might actually be under-teaching how auxiliaries are used more broadly in discourse. Having taught them in short answers at the lowest levels, they then seem to largely disappear from view. The short answers are essentially examples of ellipsis or substitution of the previous verb phrase in the question in order to avoid repetition. Using auxiliaries for substitution or ellipsis is obviously quite widespread in English, and when used in other parts of discourse, it does not necessarily carry any extra emphasis:

> A: *Have you got Josh's email?*
> B: *No, but I think Dominic has. Shall I get him to text*
> *you it?*
> A: *Could you?*
> B: *Sure. I'll do it now.*

Or

A: Has he finished the application yet?
B: No, but I wish he would. He's going to miss the deadline
if he doesn't soon.

This use of auxiliaries in ellipsis / substitution is sometimes taught in one big block at higher levels, but really it would make more sense to draw attention to it as part of our general work on tenses throughout our courses. The fact that we don't may be because typical gap-fill exercises don't really work for testing this aspect of usage. In a normal gap fill, we would give a verb in brackets and require the student to add the correct auxiliary and/or change the form of the verb. But if we also try to test the ellipsis/substitution, then it messes up the gapfill exercise:

1. I wish he ___ (finish) that application. He's going to miss the deadline.

2. A: Have you seen Paula's given up smoking?
B: Yeah, it's great. I wish Leo ___ (?!).

We can't put a prompt for the substituting *would* in number 2, for obvious reasons, but leaving the space blank doesn't work either because you are then essentially giving away the answer.

We could perhaps put 'give up' in brackets as a prompt but say in the rubric that students shouldn't use the verb if it's not necessary. However, that adds complication to the task, and many teachers and students don't like that kind of complication—which is why they don't get published very often. So if you are going to test this aspect of auxiliary use and offer a bit of challenge, you need to have a task where there is a single gap with no prompt and the student makes a choice from different auxiliary verbs. I guess that is why this area is left to an Advanced level.

Drawing attention on an on-going basis to how auxiliaries work in substitution / ellipsis therefore requires different kinds of tasks. For example, perhaps you could do it through gapping a variety of single words in a conversation or text. The gaps would be a bit like one of those FCE cloze tests that look at different bits of vocabulary and grammar (including auxiliaries).

Another possibility might be that we ask students to record a speaking task and then afterwards listen to themselves and consider where they could avoid repetition using an auxiliary only. Or perhaps we could sometimes listen out for this as the sole focus for our post-speaking feedback, using the board to show students what they said and how it could be shortened with auxiliaries.

Or maybe we should leave it entirely to fate and not focus on it at all! Sometimes caution is the better part of valour.

11

THE PRESENT CONTINUOUS

IT IS curious how grammar is sometimes divided up. For example, while most teachers nowadays are quite happy to section off *Would you like* as some kind of lexico-grammatical structure that can be taught to beginners, the low-level syllabus still dictates that *Have you been ___?* cannot be treated in this way (although ... ahem ... there are a couple of honourable exceptions, such as *Innovations Elementary* and *Outcomes Beginner*!).

In a similar way, we have split off *be going to* + verb as a unique structure entirely disconnected from (indeed, usually contrasted with) the present continuous, while the present continuous with its future meaning is separated from its use for a 'present' meaning... and often the 'present' meaning is split off between 'in progress **right now**' and 'happening **around now**'!

What's more, writers and teachers often try to find contexts that clearly fit these 'different' uses while at the same time avoiding more natural examples which may actually show that these differentiations are rather more ambiguous than they'd care to admit. I guess this is seen as being particularly important at lower levels because of the fear of confusing or overloading students.

"But ambiguity gets in the way of my teaching"

This all came into sharp focus during a discussion we had with an editor about the following box:

The present continuous (he/she/it)

We use the present continuous for activities now or at the moment (and **not** with *every day, always, usually*, etc.)

Questions

What's he studying?
Is it raining outside?
Is she coming?

Positive

She's working at home today.
He's travelling to Dubai today.
It's raining.

Negative

Her son's not feeling well.
It's not working.

The editor (or maybe the Teachers' Book writer) commented that they thought *Is she coming?* had a future meaning.

I personally didn't think so, but you be the judge. Here is the dialogue which the example comes from.

A: Where is everyone? We said 3 o'clock.
B: They're coming. Look, here's Lizzie.
C: Hi.
A: Hi Lizzie. We're waiting for everyone.
C: Yeah. They're coming. Jaime's getting coffee for everyone and Ulla is talking to someone on the phone.

B: Oh. Here's Jaime. No coffee?
D: The machine's not working!
B: Oh.
*A: And Katya? **Is she coming?***
B: No, she's working at home.
A: Oh.

Now, there is undoubtedly some ambiguity about this, and perhaps it's like one of those pictures where you either see a rabbit or a duck: it initially depends on your perception about what you see, but when the alternative is pointed out, you can actually see and accept both realities.

It is, I think, quite possible that a fluent speaker simply doesn't think about whether they are referring to the present or future, but actually just uses **Is X coming?** as a phrase to refer to a meeting that both people are / will be at!

There are three potential solutions to this example of ambiguity:

1. Re-write the dialogue.
2. Find a new context.
3. Accept the ambiguity.

Rewriting the dialogue

We could change the way the conversation is expressed to avoid the use of a present continuous – assuming you think it's a worthwhile conversation to have:

> A: *Where is everyone?*
> B: *They're here.*
> A: *Femi is in the toilet.*
> B: *Howard is in the kitchen. He wants a coffee.*

I have done something like this, for example, with a conversation about the future where we just used the simple present to avoid 'complications'. So the question there is **Do you have any plans?** and the answers stick to what the other person *wants/needs to* do. It works up to a point, but you quickly either sound a bit stupid or you simply can't go on without needing to use different forms.

Changing the context

We could change the context and what we ask students to do in order to disambiguate the meaning of the form. This is, of course, what many books do. Asking students to describe pictures or provide an example where someone is doing something different to their normal routine – such as the undercover boss in **English File**, which some of you may know.

In the first case, the result is that writers and teachers end up going down the rather odd process of describing things like some kind of voyeur: *He's taking off his jacket; She's playing the piano; They're dancing* or else they just state the bleeding obvious:

> A: *You're wearing jeans.*
> B: *You're absolutely right! I hadn't noticed.*

The other thing is that while describing can, of course, use the present continuous, it certainly doesn't have to. Things that are perceived to be complete at the moment of description can be described using the present simple – *he shoots, he scores* – and then for those of you who use videos to practise descriptions (like I used to in the past before recognising the error of my ways), you might consider how we actually describe a scene in a video in normal conversation.

We generally use the simple present all the way through unless one action is interrupted by another (i.e. essentially like narrative tenses). For example: *There's a great scene in a pub where they walk in and everyone in the pub suddenly stops talking and they turn and stare at them. And then he realises he's still wearing…* . In other words, forcing students to describe what's happening in real time with the present continuous, you may actually be practising a wrong use of the tense!

Similarly, it turns out that the context of the undercover **English File** boss mentioned above doesn't really work to provide unambiguous examples either. In the text, these are the examples designed to present the idea of now, but not always / often, etc.

> *In episode one, David Clarke, the boss of a hotel chain, is working undercover for a week in one of his hotels. He usually works in an office, but today he's working in a hotel …*
>
> **Wednesday**
>
> *Today, he's working in the restaurant. He's serving breakfast. He's wearing a uniform … the waiters always work very hard …*
>
> (from Latham-Koenig and Oxendon, **English File Beginner Students Book** Third Edition, p. 54-5. Oxford University Press)

There is, in fact, already some ambiguity in this written context. Are we reporting someone's experience (which would usually mean using the past tense) or are we reporting what happens in the episode of a TV programme, in which case we probably wouldn't use the word 'Today' or the present continuous for some of these examples. *On Wednesday, David works in the restaurant and serves … .*

But even if we accept that the context provides clear examples of the present continuous rule, what about the use of the present simple in these examples, which the article?

After the programme, David changes some things. He gives the good workers more money.

Surely, changing things and giving a pay rise is 'now and not always / often, etc.' – unless they are very lucky employees! Here, by saying it, you're showing you see the changing and giving as basically completed actions, though now I think about it, if I were in the moment of speaking, I would probably say *I'm going to change / I'm changing a few things* or *I'm giving you all a pay rise*. Wow, when you get into it, the meanings of the English tenses do start to seem pretty darned complicated.

Accepting ambiguity

Complicated? Or just fuzzy? Isn't much of the complication here actually the result of conceiving of the present continuous as having a number of entirely separate and disconnected meanings? What if we just stuck to a single meaning that encompasses all uses – how about **connected to the present (or around now) and unfinished**? Admittedly, it's a bit vague, but that is the nature of the meaning of tenses!

Which brings us to the third option: that we stick with our context and examples of waiting around for people (or whatever other natural conversation you choose). In doing so, we accept that there is potentially ambiguity in the underlying meaning of the grammar, but where we have a true natural context, these ambiguities may not even be noticed. No student – especially at this level – is ever going to question whether everyone is talking about the meeting that is about to happen or about some other future one! In the same way, if someone asks *What are you reading at the moment?* the fact that I don't have a book in my hand is a pretty clear indication that they're asking about some other reading around now.

It follows on from this that there is a real question about whether there is actually anything else to learn about the present continuous other than more examples of real usage. This might imply a somewhat different approach – for example, saying what all the examples have in common in terms of meaning or how they all relate to the core meaning. Alternatively, we might go along with Danny Norrington-Davies's idea that you simply ask students to suggest why the present continuous form is used in the particular context.

Of course, both of these previous ideas are a bit difficult if you are teaching low levels in English only, as students probably won't have the language to articulate either reasons or rules. That may also be the problem with a definition of 'connected to now and incomplete / unfinished'. Will students understand 'unfinished'? Maybe not . . . but then perhaps that might be a reason to make use of L1 (albeit briefly), which is a whole other story.

12

BE GOING

FOLLOWING on from the previous chapter on the present continuous, I pose this question – isn't *be going to* actually an example of the present continuous? This is not a new idea of mine. I don't have a copy to hand, but I think the idea was put forward in either Michael Lewis's *Meaning and*

the English Verb or R. A. Close's *A Teacher's Grammar* (to which Lewis's book owed much). If it's not there, then I'd lay the praise / blame (delete as applicable) for the notion at the feet of Jimmie Hill, the ex co-owner of Language Teaching Publications, who I used to work with!

Whatever. The reason I mention all this is because when we were putting the **Outcomes** lower-level syllabus together, we inadvertently came up against the issue of whether we should teach the present continuous for future meaning or 'be going to' because it was felt (by the publishers, by editors, by readers) that the two should never be seen together as this would only confuse students. It seems that at Beginner level, the majority of books go for the present continuous, which means we **can** teach the most common question *What are you doing . . . tonight / this weekend?* but then **can't** reply with things such as *I'm going to have lunch* or *I'm going to study*!

With **Outcomes Beginner**, we wanted to teach a future form earlier in the course than other books generally do, and were greatly encouraged to do so by **Outcomes** users in the UK who also felt it was important to do this because their students can feel socially isolated. They felt that not being prepared in class for conversations about the day ahead isn't helping these students integrate.

We had already taught the phrase *Where are you going?* in the context of someone helping a person to use a ticket machine:

A; Where are you going?
B: Lausanne.

As mentioned in our previous post, from the point of view of the knowledgeable teacher, there may be some ambiguity as to whether this is an incomplete present or a future meaning, but from the point of view of the *student*, especially the student at a basic level, given the clear context, these differences really don't matter. Accepting this, then, helps us accept that there is also ambiguity between the physical act of *going* and the signifying of an intention to do something.

Look at the examples below and try to decide which describe the (unfinished) act of movement and which signify a plan (an incomplete action!). Good luck.

A: Hey! What are you doing here?
B: I'm going to the bank.
B: I'm going to the bank to change some money.
B: I'm going to see my bank manager.
Or what about in the responses to this question?
A: What are you doing now?
B: I'm just going home.
B: I'm going for lunch.
B: I'm going to have lunch.
B: I'm going to the library to study.
B: Nothing right now, but I'm going to meet a friend at 6.

It seems to me that rather than talking about *the present continuous* and *be going to,* we could instead refer to the pattern following *'be going'* within the framework of the present continuous – though we actually don't have to formally state it as a present continuous (yet).

Here's the box / table we constructed to illustrate this pattern:

Plan	Where / what	When
	home	*now*
I'm going		
	to the gym	*this afternoon*
We're going		
	to the cinema	*at 6*
	to have a coffee	*tonight*
I'm going		
	to meet a friend	*tomorrow*
We're going		
	to see a film	*on Saturday*
	to play football	*after the class*

We go on to teach the questions:

- *What are you doing* (+ time)*?*
- *Where are you going?*
- *What time are you going?*

And we give space for students to ask other questions. Having taught a variety of question words, I think students could easily come up with the following (albeit with some 'mistakes'):

- *When are you going?*
- *Why are you going?*
- *How long are you going?*
- *How are you/we going?*
- *Who are you going?*

Clearly, this last one needs the addition of the preposition *with*. It would be up to you whether to correct this or not at this stage. I might be inclined to leave it at this point outside of just repeating and using the question correctly in my interactions with students. It is highly unlikely that students will fail to communicate what they want with 'who are you going?' – or for that matter 'who go?' – and my primary focus at this stage is to encourage and enable.

Focusing on similarity, not difference: grammar, words and meaning

Having taught the idea that *be going* can relate to a place or an action, this allows us to move on to *It's going to be nice later* or *It's going to rain*. Of course, we, as fluent speakers with a knowledge of grammar, would normally describe this as a prediction rather than a plan. But really, from the point of view of the listener, especially one with no great knowledge of grammar, is this distinction relevant or even present in their minds (indeed, is it present in the mind of *any* listener)? Obviously, it is **not** a plan in that *it, a thing, weather* or whatever don't plan stuff! So we call it something else.

The point is that this distinction isn't really inherent in *be going*, but instead it is a function of the words that go with it. The same thing happens with the individual words we teach. In his wonderful book *Lexical Analysis: Norms and Exploitations*, Patrick Hanks draws attention to how a simple meaning of a word can actually represent a variety of quite distinct processes or things. So, for example, **pulling** *a handle, a lever, a truck, his sleeve, the sticker off, me back*, etc. all represent somewhat different acts.

In other words, there is a co-construction of meaning between the words in the phrase, based on some core quality that all these different instances of ***pulling*** share, which we may not be able to precisely articulate, but which we do not question.

Isn't the same thing really happening here with *be going*? If we accept that the present continuous is 'unfinished, (temporary), connected to now', there is, as we have seen, a range of possibilities that includes meanings that are distinct – in progress before our eyes, ongoing (but not perceived at the moment of speaking), future events and a variety of in-between examples. There will be cases that are more obviously different to each other, but I'd argue that focusing on these different examples and articulating them as being separate and different is not as helpful or true as sticking to the most general meaning, drawing attention to patterns and providing lots of real-world examples.

And here's one final thought. If we want to say that *be going to* **is** a distinct form to the present continuous, how are *be* *planning to, be hoping to,* etc. distinct to the present continuous and *be going to*? And what about *be thinking of*? And if you think they are different, what makes them different (apart from the general meaning and patterns of *plan, hope* and *think)*?

And if anyone is going down the route of mentioning intentions and arrangements, you might want to read our previous chapter on future forms again!

13

VERB PATTERNS

STEP RIGHT UP... **verb patterns**! It's time for your moment in the spotlight. The word *nonsense* is perhaps a bit harsh when it comes to verb patterns, because in some ways, the rules about these patterns do simply represent facts about language. We can, for instance, definitively say that these are **not** normal patterns.

    X *I need going to the bank.*
    X *Can you moving? I can't to see.*
    X *I've started that I learn Russian.*

Terminology confusion

However, things start to go wrong when we try to **describe** the correct patterns. '*Need* is followed by an infinitive'. Or should that be 'an infinitive plus *to*'? '*Can* is followed by an infinitive'. Or should that be 'an infinitive without *to*'? With *to*, without *to*, let's call the whole thing off!

I've actually always preferred '*need* + *to* + verb' and '*can* + verb' myself, but more than one editor and grammar guru has disagreed with me. The argument is that the form after *start* or *need* is not a verb (!) in the sense that we don't say *he needs to goes to the bank*. Maybe they are right.

However, you quite often see 'verb + *-ing*' or 'the *-ing* form of the verb'. Surely this should be an 'infinitive + *ing*' if we are going to be consistent. Unfortunately, that would then lead to us saying "*start* can be followed by an infinitive or an infinitive (without *to*) + *-ing*!", which is somewhat long-winded. And what would we call the grammar point / exercise: 'infinitive or infinitive + *-ing*'? 'Verb or verb *-ing*'? Oh, to hell with it! Let's go back to 'infinitive or *-ing*'. But then…

This is something to bear in mind – and something we have seen before in these posts. Some grammar terminology is kind of created for the purpose of teaching what Scott Thornbury called a 'grammar McNugget' to study. This then means we can create form practice exercises or sorting activities to ensure students compare and contrast different points. It's also relatively easy to write an activity where we give the patterns and ask students to sort a list of verbs into the boxes of verbs followed by *-ing* and verbs followed by -inf.

Over-complication again

Then, as we continue up the levels, we're expected to expand this list of verb patterns. As we saw in our posts on continuous forms and relative clauses, there is often pressure to make grammar more complex, to give an impression of progress. And as most other grammar has already been done to death, there is plenty of scope here. Typically, the grammar is connected to 'reporting verbs', with a range of patterns such as these:

    verb + obj + *ing*
    verb + obj + inf
    verb + *(that)* + clause
    verb + *if* clause
    verb + *wh-* clause
    verb + prep + *ing*
    verb + prep + obj + *ing*
    verb + *that* + clause with subjunctive

etc.

Leaving aside the questions of whether (a) the subjunctive really exists in English and (b) we can actually describe any rules for it if it does, the bigger issue here is whether students can actually extract such 'rules' in real time when they are speaking (or even writing) – especially when you consider that many verbs will actually have more than one pattern.

Come on, we all know this idea is nonsense! So why do we continue to do it? Mainly because it's there in our books (mea culpa . . . including *Outcomes*) and they are there mainly because they are often tested via transformation exercises such as those found in the Cambridge FCE.

What value does cramming have?

So OK, for the purpose of cramming for a test, maybe there's a point, but do stop and consider how many points a student may actually gain from such cramming. At most, there may be two or three points to be gained out of 200 or more. Added to that is the fact that the most likely way for students to become accurate in the use of these verb patterns (if indeed they ever will!) is through being exposed to lots of fully grammatical examples of the verbs in action... over time... as students come across them in different contexts. We might encourage this by adding extra examples when relevant, and by eliciting (and sometimes correcting) examples from students.

Of course giving good examples is not always easy, and if you have been teaching for a long time, you might actually have been influenced by the very grammar exercises we are trying to improve upon. So when a student asks, for example, what *promise* means, many teachers will give the meaning, and write this pattern on the board:

promise to do something

and maybe give a further oral example, like *'He promised to help'*.

A variety of patterns

Don't get me wrong. I think this is better than simply saying *'promise* means X'. However, this doesn't reflect the range of ways we really use *promise*. Here are some examples from the British National Corpus based on a search for 'government promised'. I have tidied them up to make them slightly shorter and to avoid specific cultural references:

- *All last year, the government promised that talks would start soon.*
- *The government promised last year they would leave things as they were.*
- *The government promised **to publish** a regular review.*
- *In return, the government promised **to transform** the security-zones into development areas.*

- *Before the last election, the government promised an increase in public spending of £11 billion.*
- *Following international outrage, the government promised that it would change its policy.*
- *Three years ago, the government promised all food workers would be trained.*
- *The government promised **to consult** disabled people before it introduced new regulations.*
- *The government promised local residents there would be strict environmental protections.*

Teaching lexically means exposure to more grammar than focusing on rules + words does

I'm not suggesting you'd actually want to give all of these examples, but the point is that they can guide us towards giving more complete and natural examples that reflect the use and patterning of verbs. Apart from seeing here that **promised** may be followed by to + verb (or infinitive if you prefer), students may see that it can be followed by (*that*) + clause or by a noun phrase. Note that verb + clause is a very common pattern (at least in the case of *government promises*), and when seeing or hearing these kinds of examples, there are also other things students could potentially notice, such as:

- the clause after **promised** often contains **would**.
- the phrase with **promise** is often preceded by some kind of past time reference.
- various vocabulary collocations which students may

be in the process of learning such as *start soon / leave things as they were (or are) / a regular review / publish a review / change its policy*, etc.

Obviously, if we give one or two examples at the moment of teaching, this is not going to result in these patterns and collocations being acquired. It will take a number of encounters over time, but we should note that by reducing the verb pattern to a 'rule' such as *promise + infinitive / promise + clause*, we are actually reducing students' exposure to language!

This is the point about teaching lexically. By looking to constantly teach words with the grammar they're often used with, through examples, we increase the number of repeated encounters students have with 'old' words and grammar compared to what we would do if we focused more on just the grammar rule or form.

Making use of tasks and noticing patterns

Apart from giving fuller examples when we teach vocabulary, we can help students to notice verb patterns on an ongoing basis in two other ways:

- through meaningful conversation / writing tasks
- through reading / listening and tasks that encourage noticing

The tasks might be based on these words as vocabulary or something unconnected to a specific word or form. For example, students could tell (true) stories about an experience when someone, for example, **promised** them something or **accused** them of something or a time they **refused** to do something or **persuaded** someone that something was a good idea, etc.

The story may or may not include these actual verb patterns, but we can imagine other verbs with verb patterns may occur, along with lots of other grammar such as narrative tenses / reported speech. If there are errors, we can draw attention to these as we see fit either on a one-to-one basis as we go round listening and/or as part of a whole-class feedback session.

Using texts and noticing patterns

Another way we can draw attention to patterns and word grammar in texts is by doing what I call 'reverse gap-fills' after students have understood and talked about a text. The traditional way we focus on vocabulary after a text is either by matching words in the text to meanings or by providing a sentence to complete with a key word. In the 'reverse gap fill', we give the key word and have multiple gaps that focus on the grammar surrounding the word. So, say we took the examples above; we might have gaps such as the following which students complete from memory and then check by re-reading the text:

- *All last year, the government promised __ __ __ start soon.*
- *The government promised __ __ __ __ leave things as they were.*
- *The government promised __ __ a regular review.*
- *__ __, __ __ promised to transform the security-zones into development areas.*
- *__ __ __ __, the government promised __ __ __ public spending of £11 billion.*

Again, let's be clear: this is just an example based on the sentences above. With a real text, we might focus on *various* verbs as they appear, and the patterns and co-text found around them.

That's verb patterns covered then, apart from those activities where – apparently – the meaning changes when the pattern does. Now there's another fine mess we're getting ourselves into, but we'll save that delight for the next chapter!

14

MORE VERB PATTERNS

FOLLOWING on from the previous chapter on verb patterns, here's another on the same subject. You know how it is: you wait for hours for a bus and then two come along in quick succession. Not that this is a bus which you'll want to be taking, because it will take you to the hell that is the set of verbs where the verb pattern changes their meanings depending on whether they're followed by –*ing* or infinitive (with *to*... maybe).

There aren't that many of them.

The list in **Advanced Grammar in Use** is:

come, go on, mean, regret, remember, stop, try

Swan's **Practical English Usage** suggests the following can vary in meaning:

remember, forget, go on, regret, try (kind of!)*, learn and teach, stop, like* (in British English)

Learn English's list is:

like, try, stop, forget and *remember*

It's usually this last reduced list that triumphs in course-book materials, passed down from one series to the next like some kind of family heirloom that nobody really likes and that turns out to be worth precisely nothing! Why did anyone think it was of any use in the first place?

Why are you worrying about things that haven't happened yet?

The first and most important point to make about this issue is something we have seen before in these posts on grammar nonsense time and time again, and that is the creating of rules (and confusion!) in anticipation of errors that will:

1. quite possibly be never made, and
2. even if they are made, will not cause any misunderstanding in the fuller context of any given conversation.

It's a kind of neurosis to worry about things that may never happen, and it can paralyze us from doing what we want. I'd suggest the same can be true of teaching much grammar – and especially this area of grammar!

For those who have suffered the CELTA agonies of lesson planning, you'll be familiar with the concept of 'anticipated problems' connected to language analysis. Quite apart from the struggle of trying to find a list of potential problems for a piece of language you have never considered and for students you have never met, these sections are essentially creating the kinds of neuroses mentioned above. I think they also create a mindset that focuses on minutiae rather than *what students are actually trying to say.*

In class, teachers may look for the problem they anticipated rather than pay attention to students and their actual message. Or worse, they may seek out or create material that attempts to teach and encourage practice of 'rules' (because we must always practice!) to solve the supposed problem before it ever actually appears, and never allow the students to actually say anything freely!

It's like going round and unplugging everything in the morning before you leave the house while the pan you left on the stove has already caught fire! Kind of. Obviously, teaching the different forms of **try** has somewhat less dangerous consequences, but think of the hours and resources wasted on these areas. It isn't even just the grammar nuggets in our coursebooks and classes, but there are now thousands of sites and videos online. And now this blog! Can we put an end to this madness?

Distinctions without a difference

I have mentioned before how the definitions we give for forms are, at best, fuzzy and that they frequently overlap with other forms between which we are trying to draw a distinction. Take the difference between *try to do* and *try doing*. The typical definition is the one given in **Learn English**: *try to do* is 'make an attempt', while *try doing* is 'make an experiment'. In order to further 'clarify' this, it's often added that the first is 'difficult' while the second is not.

As a profession, we somehow seem to have convinced ourselves that these definitions are clear and true and our confirmation bias finds lots of examples to support our conviction. However, if we are totally honest with ourselves, this is the infamous distinction without a difference. I mean, some things you might attempt are easy for some people, and some experiments are difficult. An experiment is a kind of attempt, and an attempt is a kind of experiment (Can I do it? What will happen?). Furthermore, and despite the rules that we give, both attempts and experiments may succeed as well as fail!

In the face of this, most of the examples given in books (and no doubt by teachers) are written to fit the so-called rule. Expect to see people *trying to climb Mount Everest,* or *trying to learn to ride a bike backwards.* And they probably will add, *It's really difficult,* just in case students still don't get it.

Look at these examples:

> I **tried sending** *her flowers, writing her letters, giving her presents, but she still wouldn't speak to me.* (*Practical English Usage,* Second edition).

Is this an experiment? I know there are several things listed to make it seem that it might be, but to me, it sounds more like various attempts to apologise to a stubborn (nay, difficult!) person.

> I'm **trying to learn** *Japanese, but it's very difficult.* (*Learn English*)

Hmm. I wonder if they've ever **tried learning** Russian? That's impossible!

In whose ear does it sound 'wrong'?

So given this, how are students supposed to employ this rule accurately? Basically, they can't, and, therefore, focusing on such things and teaching the 'rules' is pointless. It's impossible to write a gap-fill for students to complete with *–ing* or infinitive after *try* where all fluent speakers would agree on the answers. I'm not saying there will be an equal number for each option, but that's the point: correctness in this case is entirely personal, a question of what *I* would say, or, more to the point, what the students' particular *teacher* would say. It's not a general truth. The same is true for distinctions between *like doing / like to do*.

Context is all

You can tell that the 'difference' in meaning for *try to like / try liking*, etc. is basically nonsense because you will find examples of both forms in the same context. At best, we can say it's a question of perspective. In the case of *mean*, *regret* and *remember*, where we can see that the forms have a clearer distinction, then the two forms will rarely appear together in a single text or conversation precisely because they have entirely different functions.

We might learn *remember* and *don't forget* + infinitive in the context of asking people to do things, but at a completely different point, learn *remember -ing* when talking about our childhoods. Similarly, *regret to do* is almost entirely a formal written formula, which is also why 'practice' of these distinctions is rubbish, because you need completely different topics and tasks!

Just to be clear here, I'm **not** saying don't teach the patterns at all. However, why do we have to bring them together? Teach the patterns separately, through examples in their appropriate context. And also understand that precisely because the contexts are so different, it's unlikely that students would confuse their different uses.

And what about the other patterns?

It's also interesting to note that the *remember + -ing* and *forget -ing* meanings are just as commonly expressed as a verb + clause!

- *Do you remember when we played that trick on the teacher?*
- *Oh, yeah. I forgot you were there too.*
- *I forgot I told you about it before.*

In fact, it's quite difficult to think of an example of *forget + -ing* other than in the chunk *I'll never forget ...-ing* . So why don't we say that the '*that* clause' patterns 'change' the meaning of these verbs (as it does in the case of *mean to do* versus *mean that...*)? We don't because that spoils our little set of verbs, our little grammar nugget. And that nugget isn't looking very meaty if we remove these verbs, and it could be even less so when you consider that...

Stop to do isn't even really a verb pattern!

As is pointed out in Swan's book, *stop to do* is actually 'stop' followed by an 'infinitive of purpose'. On this basis, we could include all kinds of other verbs as having this verb pattern, including some that also could be followed by an – *ing* form. **Go** (*go to see the bank manager / go swimming*), **write**

(*I'm writing to ask you to stop teaching differences between* **try to do** *and* **try doing**), etc. We could include this—but please don't!

Enough already!

I'm keen for everyone to give more examples of words as you teach them using the grammar which we typically use them. I'm also happy to have exercises that draw attention to patterns as they appear in actual use (as we saw with the 'reverse gap fills' in the previous chapter), but I want this to be an ongoing thing. It should just be a normal part of vocabulary learning rather than a separate grammar nugget. In fact, let's call this particular item a grammar mouldy biscuit – something indigestible that really should be thrown away! There are so many better things we could eat!

Here endeth the rant for today.

And breathe.

AFTERWORD ... IF WE MUST

There are no doubt further areas of nonsense and trauma to be encountered in the teaching of grammar which we haven't covered here. We have to accept that any attempt to impose a strict meaning on a particular kind of grammar/pattern is going to be found out sooner or later because despite our best efforts language cannot be restricted in this way. The best thing we can all do as teachers is to interrogate the rules we have been given and that we give, and when they are found wanting, try not to perpetuate them. It is not inevitable that things stay as they are.

There was a time when much was made of the difference between *must* and *have to*. You will no doubt see this still in notes such as this one from *English File Pre-intermediate* (2005):

Must and have to are very similar, but there is a small difference.
We normally use have to for a general obligation (a rule at work or
law). We usually use must when the speaker imposes the obligation
(for example, a teacher to students or a parent to children). But
often you can use either. (p. 134)

However, the **exercises** that focus on practice avoid any opportunity to **test** this rule. They instead focus on the correct form of *have to* and making choices between *have to, don't have to* and *mustn't*. These are choices based on clear unambiguous distinctions.

The latest edition of Michael Swan's *Practical English Usage* (2016) – a fully revised *International* Edition (OUP's emphasis) – also retains this distinction but now adds that in American English this difference really doesn't exist and increasingly it doesn't in British English either.

One could argue that given this fact, it seems a bit pointless to even to mention there is a distinction anywhere, let alone give over half a page to it!

Still, I think we have to see this as progress. It is very difficult to give up on long-held beliefs and effectively admit that we were wrong! There are many teachers in this situation – they have studied hard, learned the rules and passed State exams to prove it. Understandably, they can be resistant to the idea that learning these 'rules' was a waste of time. Publishers, understandably, don't want to disappoint these people, maybe because they're commercially minded, but maybe also because they want to respect the effort those teachers have put in.

The formula we see here is basically, 'Here's what people have said – you (teachers) were right – but basically you (students) can forget about it!' It's also a reasonable signal for other teachers, who for whatever reason are open to change, to simply ignore the whole thing and focus on meanings and forms where they can provide some certainty or clarity.

Who knows? Maybe in the next editions of these books, these references will have disappeared entirely. And ELT will be better for it.

BOOKS AND REFERENCES

This is not an academic book. As stated in the forward, these chapters were very much written as rants, for amusement as much as education. As such, you will not find rigorous Harvard referencing. Direct quotes are referenced in text, but not here. I have sometimes taken examples from coursebooks. Where there is reference to a text/lesson or an extended quote, these are referenced with a year to indicate the edition that is being referred to – which was the edition I had to hand. These may be different in newer editions.

Below is a further reading list. Think of these as retweets – books or articles that have sparked thoughts or made me aware of something, but not necessarily representing my actual views or endorsed by us.

~

Ken Paterson, Rebecca Sewell and Caroline Caygill

A Handbook of Spoken English (Klett/Delta Publishing 2018)

This is the book I mentioned in my introduction. Personally, the benefit has come from my discussions with the authors who were colleagues for many years at the University and have remained friends. It offers a very accessible route into Spoken Grammar for teachers and students alike. Generally, it presents examples of patterns and opportunities to put them into practice rather testing 'correctness'.

∼

Martin Parrot

Grammar for English Language Teachers Cambridge University Press, 2006

As mentioned, in the chapter on indirect questions, but not confined to that chapter, I generally like Martin Parrot's approach to grammar. He generally seeks to find unifying themes (though not quite to the extent of Lewis below) and the avoidance of lots of lists of exceptions and unnecessary rules. He has a light academic style, which is looking for clarity rather than show of how clever he is.

∼

Michael Swan

https://mikeswan.net/articles/

Practical English Usage hardly needs any introduction, and I have a copy, which I look at occasionally even if I don't agree with it always – as noted in the text of this book.

Rather than his grammar books, I would more strongly recommend checking out Mike's articles which are available on his website. They reveal someone whose attitude to grammar is somewhat different to the reputation of a 650-page grammar book. They may be summed up as explanations should have a very minor role and grammar is a varied thing which should be focused on and practised in varied ways. A view I wholeheartedly endorse. Plus, he's a very clear and witty writer.

$\sim$

Ron Carter and Michael McCarthy

The Cambridge Grammar of English (CUP 2006)

English Grammar: Your Questions Answered (Prolinguam Publishing, 2017)

To be fair, I'd say Carter and McCarthy have had a bigger influence on me through their teaching and conference presentations than anything. You can find various presentations on YouTube. Together and separately, they have written a a lot on spoken grammar as something which is real, present, and teachable. Their reference book promotes this. It's not maybe the most accessible reference, but you can decide.

The second book is a short ebook aimed more at native speakers and fluent non-native users than students or teachers. It gives answers to the kinds of questions we get on English Questions Answered. If you just want to read the introduction though on Amazon, it gives a wonderful explanation of what grammar is and what it's not.

∾

Pawley and Syder

Two puzzles for linguistic theory: nativelike selection and nativelike fluency

available at: https://lextutor.ca/rt/pawley_syder_83.pdf

This is the seminal article that really underpins some of the ideas we discuss here and in many of the lexically orientated books and descriptive grammar cited here. Grammar may be potentially infinitely generative and flexible, but in practice it's not used like that.

∾

Scott Thornbury

Natural Grammar: The Key Words of English and How They Work (Oxford 2004)

I personally think the book as somewhat flawed as a self-study book, in that it's unclear what level of student might use it, and a whole page might be too much information and practice. However, it does offer a really important example of how we could view language and grammar differently. Individual features or exercises of the words covered may also provide some nice grammar olives.

~

Michael Lewis

The English Verb (Cengage Learning, 1986)

The Lexical Approach (Cengage Learning, 1993)

As I mentioned in the text, I think I went slightly down the wrong track for a while with my teaching after by Michael Lewis's book on the English verb. But I think really the issue was more in my application rather than the actual thesis, which aims to identify simple unifying rules for the verb tense system. You will have seen that idea has definitely percolated into my thinking here (see "Present Continuous" and "Be Going").

Maybe he had some change of heart about the practice too, who knows, but his next book was *The Lexical Approach*, which refocused attention on vocabulary and grammatical-ising lexis.

~

Dave Willis (with Jane Willis)

Winning the Grammar Wars (Willis-elt, 2015)

Again, this ebook is more about the situation in the UK regarding attitudes towards grammar and how it is taught. I think it highlights the point I made in the chapter on the word grammar itself. People's attitudes towards learning grammar in a foreign language are often influenced by a political discourse about language that is ongoing in society. This is a passionate polemic written with rather greater knowledge and academic rigour than I have!

~

There's more ... but I think that's enough to be getting on with.

ABOUT THE AUTHORS

Lexical Lab (https://www.lexicallab.com) was founded by Hugh Dellar and Andrew Walkley in 2014. They previously worked together at the University of Westminster for 17 years, which is where they first met. Lexical Lab provides high quality teacher training and English language development focused on *Teaching Lexically*.

Teaching Lexically encourages students to take part in genuine communication and encourages teachers to provide language to support it. But *Teaching Lexically* also recognises that communication and language development are essentially lexically driven and that grammar is best acquired as lexis and through vocabulary teaching.

We provide face-to-face courses abroad, a summer school in London and now a variety of online offerings. We also write coursebooks, methodology and develop other material through our website and partners.

Andrew and Hugh have written the following books together:

- With National Geographic Learning (formerly Thomson/Cengage Learning) they have written two coursebook series, *Innovations* and *Outcomes* (currently in its second edition) plus the Upper Intermediate level of *Perspectives*.
- With Pearson they wrote the B1+ and B2+ students' books for the series *Roadmap*.
- With Klett (formerly DELTA publishing), they wrote the methodology book, *Teaching Lexically*.

∽

Andrew Walkley has been in ELT for 30 years now. He has worked in Spain as well as the UK and has conducted talks, workshops, and short courses in around 30 countries around the world. Outside of teaching he keeps fit through running, playing football, and long walks. He has an allotment where he grows vegetables – and a lot of weeds. He enjoys reading – both fiction (favourite author: Anne Tyler) and non-fiction. He cooks, he cleans, he watches TV, and he likes a kip in the afternoon.

∽

Hugh Dellar has over twenty-five years' experience in ELT – English Language Teaching – and is the co-founder of the online school and training company **Lexical Lab**. He has co-authored two five-level General English series, **Outcomes** and **Innovations,** both published by National Geographic Learning, as well as one level of the high-school series **Perspectives**. His first methodology book, **Teaching Lexically**, came out via Delta Publishing in 2016. Most recently, he has worked on two levels of the new Pearson General English series, **Roadmap**. In addition, he is a life-long Arsenal supporter, obsessive hoarder of obscure 1960s vinyl, keen reader, and general bon viveur, as the photo bears witness to!

www.ingramcontent.com/pod-product-compliance
Lightning Source LLC
Chambersburg PA
CBHW060807050426
42449CB00008B/1577